The
Kenning
Collection

Compiled by

A. Vaughan

GUILD PUBLISHING
LONDON

This edition published 1985 by
Book Club Associates
By arrangement with
Oxford Publishing Co.

Printed in Great Britain by
Netherwood Dalton & Co. Ltd, Huddersfield, Yorks.

Introduction

I hope you will find this collection of William Lovell Kenning's photographs interesting. They include engines from the London, Brighton and South Coast Railway, the South Eastern and Chatham Railway, the Midland and Great Northern Joint Railway, and of course the one and only Great Western Railway. All the south country railways featured were recorded in 1913 and 1914, while the northern companies' engines date from 1920 when Bill Kenning, Surrey born and Berkshire educated, was serving with his regiment, the Royal Scots Fusiliers.

A remarkable aspect of these photographs is the vantage points from which they were taken. Most people would agree that discipline on the railway was stricter in the period of these pictures than it has been since, yet Bill, at only 14 years of age was allowed to move freely over the railway. Either discipline was not strict in 1914 or Bill had at an early age the persuasive talents which I came to know so well fifty years later.

I feel that a great deal of the strictness we associate with working life fifty years ago was really the self discipline of a worker who had pride in his achievements. The engines would not have looked so sparkling if the only incentive for a man to work was fear of the "sack". It was this pride that allowed Bill access to forbidden places; if some crusty old driver who drove his "own" engine knew that Bill too loved the green and copper machine, he would be delighted to allow the young lad onto the footplate just to show off his beloved engine and have it admired.

At the time these photographs were taken, locomotives had their "regular" driver, who in turn had a "regular" fireman, and this tri-partite alliance, keeping fairly close to a daily routine of work, became thoroughly practised in the art of running the train to time as economically as possible. On shed too, this regularity had great value in that the locomotive was serviced by the same group of cleaners and fitters, firedroppers and steam raisers.

There is no doubt that a loyalty, or affection, sprang up where a driver had his "own" engine, and because of this it could be kept running on crack expresses long after its class had been superceded by more powerful types. The "single wheeler" *Worcester* was driven by one regular driver for some years. In passing it is worth noting that this man played the organ during Sunday service in Worcester Cathedral, and within a month of this driver's retirement the engine was withdrawn from service. It was old, most of its fellows had already been scrapped, and once its driver, who spent a lot of his spare time maintaining it, had retired, the obsolete engine had to be retired too. It was not unusual for men to come into the shed on their days off to carry out repairs and adjustments or simply to do some burnishing; some men were so proud of their engines that they used to take the regulator handle home with them to prevent anyone moving their locomotive, or so the story goes.

Cleaners, starting at thirteen or fourteen were first put to work on the tender wheels, graduating to the tender water tank, the engine's wheels, boiler cladding and finally to the copper and brass work. Before 1914 it was usual to have large numbers of boys cleaning each engine, sometimes as many as twenty where a big express engine was concerned. To keep soot and smuts from the brass and paint-work they made covers from sacking, properly shaped to fit each part, and the foreman often had to get into a bad temper before these earliest of enthusiasts could be removed from an engine so that it could go off shed to take up its working — no wonder these engines gleamed like glass case models!

After five or six years, during which they cleaned every rod and chain on the engine, they had acquired a comprehensive knowledge of the anatomy of a variety of locomotives which was to be the basis for all the rest of their training. Besides gaining practical knowledge, they also acquired a repertoire of practical jokes, some of which were harmless like putting a running hose up the trouser leg of a colleague and some dangerous like locking a man in the firebox. If stays or tubes inside the firebox needed attention, the work was often carried out with the engine still in steam, though of course the fire would be drawn before the man got inside, but it was still a dreadfully hot place and a terrifying prison. At this period there were always a few clean, dry tenders standing around, as once a month each engine's tender had to be cleaned inside and out, the coal space being white-washed to show that it *was* clean and in these the young cleaners could hide from the foreman while they played cards or simply slept. It must be remembered that the twelve hour day was in force at this time. Taking advantage of these "slackers", other cleaners would drop lighted, oily waste into the tank, weight the lid, and then those outside would fall about in hysterics listening to the frantic panic sounding faint and hollow inside the iron tank.

High spirits and rough spirits separated as the boys grew older, and they channelled their energies away from silly tricks and into the enthusiastic study of locomotive matters. The complications of the vacuum brake, and the diagnosis of faults from the peculiar rhythms heard in the exhaust from the chimney, were just two of the many studies that had to be mastered before a fireman could become an engine-driver. If a man wanted to rise to the top of the profession, he had to be self-disciplined and responsible as well as enthusiastic; in this connection it is well to recall how many drivers have become civic officials such as Mayors, Aldermen, Members of Parliament and Justices of the Peace. It is difficult to imagine these steady, solemn looking men "thrashing" an engine, and yet, when occasion required they "tucked their beards into their overalls" and produced the most amazing feats of haulage from unlikely engines. The *Cornish Riveria*, a five hundred ton train, has been hauled between Reading and London by two Armstrong 0-6-0 freight engines, at speeds in excess of sixty miles an hour, and the same train, hauled by a 31XX tank has kept time between Westbury and London. In 1914 this sort of running was regarded as "thrashing", a practise frowned upon yet tolerated by authority, as it enhanced the prestige of the line through the wonderful speeds obtained, and got them out of a hole by getting a train in on time and thus saving much adverse criticism.

By 1964 the concept of "thrashing" had largely been forgotten for a variety of reasons. The War had shown that a steam engine would run quite well without all the "molly-coddling" it had been used to receiving, and anyhow they were on the way out and were expendable, so to speak. Thus in the last few years of steam on the Western Region we saw such feats of running as had never been seen before, when drivers had one last "fling" before settling down to their artless diesels.

I was constantly amazed at steam engine performance during the first half of the sixties. Working in the signal box, I had plenty of opportunity to observe the running. There was the 61XX on the

7.45 a.m. Didcot—Swindon stopper keeping time with fourteen coaches on a three coach schedule, or the 49XX, standing in for a failed "Hymek", hauling four hundred and fifty tons "all stations" to Reading and then fast to Paddington *making up* time where the rostered diesel would have been hard pressed to keep time. This happened several times and at least one Didcot driver has a letter of thanks from the General Manager for completing such a run. The roll of honour is very long, but one day it will be written down properly and credit given where it is due.

The steam engine demanded, or persuaded, the men to do their best. It created loyalty to the Company and pride in the job, and not just for enginemen, but for signalmen, porters and everyone else. Non-railwaymen may find this difficult to believe but it is true. Even signal and telegraph technicians (God bless them) have said that the railway has lost its spirit since the steam engines finished. If, as a signalman you delayed a "King" or a "Castle" on some express, (even if through no fault of your own), your guilty feelings as it came storming past, with driver glaring, and fireman digging to replace the fire going out of the chimney with the blast, were far better than all the admonitions of Inspectors in ensuring that you were more careful in future!

In future the railway will be "pre-packed" so to speak, as locomotives, signalling and track maintenance becomes increasingly mechanised or automated. As this new movement develops so the sense of satisfaction that a railwayman received from his work will diminish. Already a locomotive crew cannot pat themselves on the back for a job well done as they have little to do with how fast their train runs, since they merely sit down and "turn on the tap".

I am grateful for the opportunity to record how the old time railwaymen felt about their work, and to register my eternal admiration for the men who, with "inefficient" signalling and "inefficient" locomotives, running on track laid entirely by hand and maintained without any mechanical aids, managed to run a railway twice or even three times as busy as it is today. By pride in their work, in their personal skills, they overcame obstacles which seem to us enormous, rising to peaks of efficiency and public service which will I feel never be seen again. It appears sadly inevitable that as we find ways of performing work more comfortably, so the work becomes less interesting and therefore less satisfying mentally. One can justifiably look back at the periods pre-war and earlier and call them the "good old days".

No. 2913 *Saint Andrew* stands magnificently at No. 1 platform Paddington on the 4 p.m. to Chester and Birkenhead on the 19th September 1913. These engines were considered by many enginemen to have been the finest express locomotives on the Great Western, having all the virtues that were later to make Staniers "Black 5's" famous. To quote one veteran engine driver, they could "steam like a witch", a curious analogy, but they certainly were prodigious steam raisers, and even with sixteen coaches they could keep the fastest schedules, requiring speeds of over 70 mph. No doubt this sort of running was not achieved without a good deal of effort on the fireman's part, but the point that the men appreciated was that the engine always responded to their efforts. On a late running train, two determined men and a Saint made a formidable alliance.

Not just a "Star" but a whole constellation, *The Great Bear* was the pride of small boys and the Company's publicity department. Enginemen felt differently however as the locomotive was hard on its firemen. There were two problems – the boiler did not raise steam freely and the fire was difficult to feed owing to the thoughtless design of a simple thing like the firehole door. The fire-grate was very wide, requiring the fireman to throw the coal sideways, and the comparative narrowness of the firehole (it was the same size as that in the "Stars" but with a larger grate) prevented him from properly covering the extreme edges of the fire-bars. Thus the fire grew thin at those points, allowing cold air to enter the fire-box, lowering the temperature and so reducing still further the steam raising capabilities of the boiler. Of course, Old Oak men mastered the job, but an engine that is "shy" for steam *and* awkward to fire was never likely to make a reputation for fast running.

The noble front end of No. 2936 *Cefntilla Court* at Paddington in 1913. The headlamps do not appear to be positioned properly over the buffers, nor are they equi-distance from the edge of the buffer beam. Looking through these and other photographs I see that the positioning of lamps does tend to vary as in the picture on page 13.

An unusual view of No. 103 *President* with driver Harry Goldsworthy, standing at Radley in Oxfordshire on a Paddington to Oxford stopping train in July 1915. These engines, known as the "Frenchmen" because of their country of origin, were popular with their crews because they steamed freely and rode smoothly, even at high speed. The engines worked hard, filling in time between fast Oxford—Paddington passenger train workings with stopping trains from Oxford to Reading or Swindon. As there were only three of these unusual engines on the line, and all of them shedded at Oxford, there was much friendly rivalry between the enginemen who regularly drove them as to whose engine was the cleanest. When the opportunity arose, shed staff would line the three engines together so that comparative inspections could be made. A good deal of leg pulling and good natured criticism took place on these occasions all of which contributed to the cameraderie and morale of everyone concerned.

Although not one of Churchward's masterpieces, the "County" class 4-4-0's ran considerable mileages before being broken up. This one, No. 3828 *County of Hereford*, was built in 1912 and cut up in 1933, having covered over three quarters of a million miles. The location is on the up middle road at Oxford where it is waiting to take over a southbound express. These engines were employed on cross-country services at this time so the engine is possibly waiting for a Sheffield to Bournemouth connection, this almost certainly hauled by a Great Central "Atlantic".

This photograph was taken soon after 5353 had left the factory, brand new, in August 1918. The engine is coupled to clerestory stock in the "Marlborough" bay at Swindon and is probably acting as station pilot as part of its "running in" duties. The reverser is in the back gear position, and the driver is checking his watch, probably to see how long before he has to wait before he can move off to the carriage sidings. The engine is of a slightly different design from the original conception, the frames having been lengthened by nine inches to give more room for the "plumbing" under the footplate. A new cast iron chimney (similar in profile to the earlier copper capped one) is fitted and there is a sloping guttering above the cab side sheets. These engines were always popular, being used on fast freights and secondary passenger duties, as between Gloucester and Hereford, or over the old M. & S.W.Jct. route. Those shedded at Weymouth worked daily to Paddington on expresses of ten or eleven coaches at speeds in excess of seventy m.p.h. The 43XX class, designed by G. J. Churchward, scored yet another first for the G.W.R. — the first mixed traffic 2-6-0 in the country and one of the most successful.

A very rare sight is this 43XX covered in wartime grime, on the up main line, about to pass Kennington Junction with an "H" headcode freight. Another unusual point is that the signalman has been quick to replace his home signal. Normally they were left "off" until the train was well past so as to avoid worrying the driver should he look back and see the signal at "danger". Notice also that a 2-4-0 tender engine has just left the loop tender first for Oxford.

One of the first batch of 43XX's. seen here working hard on a freight train passing Abingdon Road Halt on the up main during 1915. The engine was fully lined out with the "Garter" coat of arms on the tender and a handsome copper capped chimney. What a marvellous sight she must have been.

An Armstrong Class 0-6-0 freight engine, No. 455 is about to pass Kennington Junction on the down main line. At this time this class was known as the "Old Standard Goods", having been superceded in the role of goods engine by the highly successful Dean engines. The Armstrongs were by no means eclipsed however and at the period of this picture, some thirty years after the design was introduced, the class could still give a good performance. There was a working from Shrewsbury to Chester for one of these engines which gave it the work of three engines — pick-up goods to Chester, a stopping passenger from Chester to Birkenhead and back, and then a Chester to Paddington restaurant car express, which it took back to Shrewsbury at over 60 mph. before handing over to a "Star" or a "Saint". They should have been called the "Ever Readies" because even unprepared engines have been known to haul the "Cornish Riveria" (all 14 coaches of it) from Reading to Paddington at speeds of around 60 mph.

This is not, I'm afraid a very good photograph, but I included it for the historical interest. In 1866 Joseph Armstrong designed a standard locomotive, varying the wheel arrangement and diameter to achieve a passenger or a freight engine. The locomotive in the picture was a "Sir Daniel" class 2-2-2, 7 ft single wheeler, but when the train loads became too heavy for its limited adhesion, it was a simple matter to convert it to an 0-6-0 standard goods. As the boiler, cylinders, motion and most other parts were common to both classes, all that was necessary was to reposition the "horns" to take the altered wheel arrangement and to change the inclination of the cylinders. The result was, to all intents and purposes, a "388" class except for the curved framing over the centre driver where the big wheel had been. This engine is seen hauling an up train past Kennington Junction.

No. 2341, a Dean "Standard Goods" is proving here the versatility of the breed by hauling a train of eight wheelers, probably on the Oxford—Thame branch. Like their forebearers, the old standard goods, these little engines were terrific steam raisers, and though fitted with small driving wheels, they were quite happy on passenger train duties. During the period of the Great War, Weymouth shed used two of this class for working special passenger trains to Bristol. This was when the train was routed over the Radstock line and an engine with a light axle loading was needed in consequence. The load was often eight coaches, a heavy one when you think of the 1 in 50 climb to Dorchester and the incredible switchback from Frome through Farrington Gurney to the junction with the main line at North Somerset Junction. A "double home" working for a Weymouth "2301" was to take the evening freight all the way to Oxley, returning next night with more freight.

An unidentified "Duke" about to leave Oxford on an up stopping passenger train. The smokebox door is of an early design with a stiffening ring on the periphery. Ten years earlier this would have been brightly polished steel (see photographs of Broad Gauge engines in particular). Just ahead of the engine one can see a "fouling bar" which is a pre-track circuiting device to prevent the signalman moving the facing points as a train is going over them.

Compare this cab with that of No. 3445 *Flamingo* on page 18 and the standardisation of GWR locomotives will be readily appreciated. Differences are only ones of size, except that this engine, No. 4026 *King Richard* had no steam brake, but the more modern four cone ejector with the vacuum brake working on the engine. The driver's hand is resting on the brake handle and the ejector control can be seen behind his forearm. You will notice that there is no "small ejector" handle. This was a tap admitting steam to only one of the four cones, thus keeping the brakes off with a minimum consumption of steam, but this picture is too early to show this modification. Another slight difference between this cab and the ones that I was used to is the reversing screw handle. In my days the notches were covered over, but here they are uncovered — a trap for unwary fingers.

The cab of No. 3445 *Flamingo*, a "Bulldog" 4-4-0. On the right is Driver Webb, a man who suffered from migraine headaches, surely the worst kind of illness one could have on a noisy, vibrating steam engine. To the right of Webb's shoulder there is the combined steam and vacuum brake control. The handle opened a valve to admit air to the vacuum pipe, while the curly pipe from the right led air to the round box at the top of the apparatus wherein was housed a piston. The air lifted the piston (because a vacuum existed above it) causing steam to enter the steam brake cylinder, as seen in the picture on page 21. Thus the force applied to the steam brake on the engine was in direct proportion to the force applied to the vacuum brakes on the train. No fire is visible in this picture because the plate which Bill Kenning used to make the negative was not sensitive to red. The engine is in "Mark's Hole" sidings outside Oxford goods shed signal box, known today as Oxford Station South.

This is the best of the negatives I have showing No. 3702 *Halifax*. As there are several in the collection I would be inclined to think that these men were particular friends of Bill. No. 3702 is seen here standing at Radley on a down stopping passenger train to Oxford.

A "517" class No. 522 seen here at Radley around 1916. These were remarkable little engines, doing all the work that a diesel rail car does today, as well as the shunting. During the period of this photograph, there was at Weymouth a certain Driver Nutty who drove an engine of this class on stopping passenger trains to Yeovil. This was just over twenty seven miles of switch-back road, with many of the stops on 1 in 50 rising gradients, and between stops speed had to rise to 45 mph. if time was to be kept. All this suggests that there was a lot of main valve and long cut-off driving, yet the engine was very economical at about 35 lbs. of coal per mile. Driver Nutty did a lot of his own maintenance, coming to work on his days off, and it is said that one of his checks for the engine was to push it from the shed *by hand,* to ensure that she was nicely balanced on the wheels and turning freely!

No. 1972 was converted from saddle to pannier tank and is seen here standing at Paddington with a train of empty stock. Tank engines were not commonly used for stock working during this period, but a system was in force similar to the one used at Paddington today, where the big express engines bring in empty coaches and take out a loaded train later. This engine has a "garter" coat of arms and a copper capped chimney. Notice behind the chimney is a working distant signal suspended from the station roof. The engine's wheels are unusual Swindon practice in that they have "I" section spokes similar to the Webb "coal-tanks" of the L.N.W.R. One can just see the steam brake cylinder and piston rod behind the cab footsteps, whilst the bunker carries the usual tank engine clutter of fire-irons and buckets. The figure "9" is the trip number, an identifying mark to help signalmen route the engine properly. A "weather sheet" is rolled up on top of the cab, which in wet weather was stretched in tent fashion across to the irons one can see standing in the bunker.

No. 3629 seems to me to have a slightly comical look about it. She is the last but one of a class which could hardly have departed further from standard G.W.R. practice. It was a copy of the L.N.W.R. and L. & Y.R. 2-4-2 tank, with Webb radial axle boxes, an enclosed cab and steam operated water scoop. None of the features so far mentioned had been seen on the G.W.R. before. The boiler was a shortened version of that fitted to the "Camel" class 4-4-0. Earlier engines of the batch had their piston valves placed one above the other, between the cylinders. The top one feeding steam to the left hand cylinder; distortion due to heating caused trouble and this engine was fitted with slide valves. The class were not good steamers and this engine was fitted with a blast pipe, petticoat and diaphragm of Great Central design! She is seen here at Kidlington with Stationmaster Cook and other railwaymen.

A copper capped "28XX" class, No. 2813, with a Southall to Bordersley Junction freight about to pass Radley. The "28's" were probably one of the most powerful freight locomotives in the country, with the exception of the Beyer-Garratts from 1903 until the advent of the B.R. 92XXX class 2-10-0's in 1960. They were the first engines in the country to haul a load in excess of 2,000 tons when, in April 1906, No. 2808 took 109 wagons on test from Swindon to Acton. No. 2808's load amounted to 2012 tons, and it must be remembered that the rolling resistance of those ancient wagons was far greater than that of the wagons hauled by the diesel. After the test it was stated that 2808 had worked 25% below full capacity and burned six pounds of coal per d.b.h.p.h.

This picture shows a Great Central Railway "Atlantic" No. 264 standing at the down platform Oxford with the 7.45 am. Southampton—York express on the 14th May 1914. With looks like these the Robinson "Atlantics" could never have remained class C.4 for long. They soon took the name of a beautiful Edwardian entertainer and were known to everyone as "Jersey Lilies". The high regard in which they were held stemmed from more than mere looks, for they steamed freely and ran very fast on the expresses between Marylebone and Sheffield, sweeping down the long Chiltern gradients at speeds of up to 90 mph., storming the Pennines and responding to the fireman's best efforts as he dug steadily to keep the boiler pressure at maximum.

Ex-L.B.S.C.R. No. 75 *Blackwall*, now No. 9 of the Isle of Wight Central Railway, waiting at Newport with a train for Sandown via Merstone and Newchurch. This engine, built in 1872, was sent to the Island in 1899 and completed twenty-eight years more work before being withdrawn in 1927.

This Beyer-Peacock 2-4-0 (No. 5 built 1876) tank looks, if anything, more antiquated than No. 9 on page 25. In fact this 2-4-0 is the younger by four years. This picture shows it at Newport, safety valves roaring as the driver gives it a last check before setting out on the long run to Ventnor Town over a route that crosses the high central downland of the Island on gradients of 1 in 60 — a tough job for a little engine. Number five is fitted with a Westinghouse air compressor (seen just in front of the water tanks) as the train's brakes are operated by air pressure, artificially created instead of the usual vacuum system. Needless to say, British Rail are now fitting all their modern stock with compressed air brakes.

The initials F.Y.N. on the tank side are not enough to disguise an L.B.S.C.R. engine. Built at Brighton in 1876 as No. 46 *Newington* of the "A.1" class, it subsequently became L.S.W.R. No. 734. It worked on the Lyme Regis branch in 1903, before coming to the Freshwater, Yarmouth and Newport Junction Railway in 1913. Its arrival on the Island was due to a quarrel between the F.Y.N. and the company supplying engines and coaches to work the Isle of Wight Central. Thirty six years later this engine returned to the mainland as B.R. 32646 where it gave a few more years of useful service.

Bill was on his way to the Longmoor Railway when he took this picture of Adams 4-4-2T tank No. 428 somewhere on the Bordon branch. The engines of this class "415" were supplied by Beyer-Peacock in 1882 and, although built to Adams designs, they plainly bore the Beyer look. Compare this engine with the one on page 33. For many years they were the standard suburban passenger tanks for the L.S.W.R. They were very economical and could accomplish a great deal of work on the one thousand gallons of water carried in the side tanks. Like all the Adams engines they were elegant movers (one can be seen at work on the Bluebell Railway), and although some people prefer them to carry their original "stovepipe" chimney, others like them better with the Drummond "flare-top" as shown here.

An Adams "X2" class standing "light" at Woking. This elegant machine is the result of constant modification to an original design introduced in 1880. Like their predecessors they worked the fastest trains. There was a large-wheeled and a small-wheeled version for work on the flat and hilly sections of the line. The "T6" was the large, 7'1" engine. The locomotive appears to be in its original form with the exception of the "flare-top" Drummond chimney. Dugald Drummond left his predecessors' designs alone but he could not abide the Adams "stove-pipe" chimney and replaced as many as he could.

The "D15" class, of which No. 470 shown here, as rebuilt by Urie with superheater, and the firebox water tubes removed, was probably the most powerful 4-4-0 locomotive that Drummond built for the L.S.W.R. A big free-steaming boiler supplied the two 20″ x 26″ cylinders. These drove wheels six feet seven inches in diameter to such good effect that the engines became firm favourites with the crews of the heavy Waterloo—Bournemouth and Waterloo—Exeter expresses. No. 470 is seen here at Salisbury during the period of the First World War.

Dugald Drummond designed this engine, a far cry from the sturdy simplicity of his "T9"s, and "D15"s. We see here a member of the "E10" class, 4-2-2-0, an engine as curious as its wheel arrangement suggests. There were four cylinders, the two inside working on the leading wheels, while the outside two drove the trailing wheels. Steam was supplied to the inside cylinders by Stephenson's valve gear and by Joy's gear to the outside. Both sets of valve gear were controlled from one screw in the cab, and to complete this unorthodox arrangement the driving wheels were not coupled. This often resulted in the trailing wheels slipping round madly when the engine was starting, while the leading wheels gripped and turned slowly! All the latest aids to steam raising and thermal efficiency were included, such as cross firebox water tubes and feed-water heater. Despite all this the engines were not a success and only worked trains when "Nine Elms" were short of locomotives. They could run fast but were poor steam raisers which of course restricted their usefulness. The class was introduced in 1901 and the last one was scrapped in 1927. No. 371 is seen here at Woking.

A Midland and Great Northern Joint Railway engine No. 80, is seen here running into South Lynn station probably to pick up a holiday train during 1910. Notice the tender piled high with coal ready for a long run, and the fine gantry under which the engine is passing. These were the "crack" engines of the line, hauling heavy loads of holiday-makers over the miles of single track railway which comprised the M. & G.N. Jt. Railway. To assist fast running, a token catcher was fitted to the tender side near the cab, thus allowing the driver to keep up a higher speed while collecting the token which would normally have been taken up by hand. The engines are obviously of Midland Railway origin, elegant if somewhat antiquated, and were in fact designed by S. W. Johnson at Derby and built by the firm of Beyer Peacock No. 4072 in 1899, the M. & G.N. purchasing them soon afterwards. They worked on this line, on the heaviest work, for forty years.

Another Beyer-Peacock 4-4-0, No. 21 on the M. & G.N. Jt. running into Melton Constable.

How are the mighty fallen! One of Mr. Stirling's famous "Eight Foot Singles", heroes of the incredible "Race to the North", legendary in their exploits on long distance expresses, now in the last few years of its life. It was delegated to working slow stopping trains from Peterborough when this photograph was taken sometime before 1915.

An "F" class 4-4-0, otherwise known as a "Jumbo", not because of its size but as a term of affection. The class was built to haul the "Dover Mail" and other important expresses on the South Eastern Railway. This particular engine came out of Ashford Works in 1898 and ran until 1933, though by that time it was no longer employed on "crack" trains but used mainly for secondary routes like the Reading to Redhill line. It was on this line that No. 185 was photographed at Blackwater, on the 2.22 p.m. from London Bridge to Reading. The photograph was taken after Spring 1916 but possibly during the First World War — note what appears to be a fitting on the front of the tender to fix the tarpaulin from the cab, an ARP precaution in that war.

A re-built "Jumbo", or "F.1" class, on the 4.10 pm. Reading—Redhill with Driver J. Tugwell looking out. This picture and the one on page 35 show plainly how an engine's looks can be improved by the substitution of a short chimney for a long one and a "fatter" boiler. The original tender is still in use, indeed these ancient vehicles were still in tow behind veteran locomotives on this route in 1950. This photograph was taken after 1916.

Proving the versatility of the "C" class (built 1904), No. 272, built in the 1880's as a freight engine is seen here at South Croydon on a race special, Epsom to St. Paul's.

A Stirling "O" class rebuilt in 1914 to class "O1" as depicted by 0-6-0, No. 369, the mount of driver J. Ider, which stands under the signal gantry at Caterham. Both engine and gantry had a long life, as the author remembers them both working in 1951 and 1952 respectively.

Besides being a photograph of No. 369 (as in picture No. 38), here is a good close-up of an S.E.C.R. bracket signal. Notice that this railway favours white dots on the signal arms instead of the more usual white rectangles. It is difficult to understand the thinking behind this because a white rectangle shows clearly from a distance whether the arm is raised or lowered but the dot gives no such help.

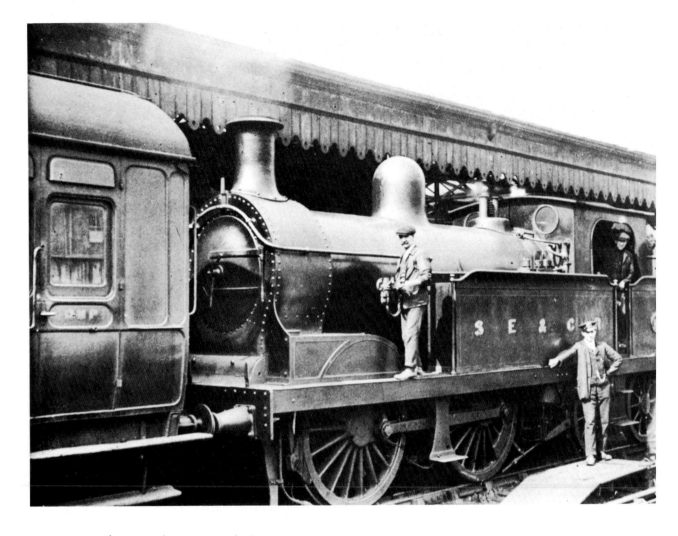

A *Stirling* "Q" class 0-4-4T rebuilt in 1914 to "Q1" 0-4-4 tank No. 363 photographed shortly after its rebuilding in 1914. When first built, in 1891, it had a tall chimney, but now the engine looks sturdy and business-like with its stumpy funnel. The photo was taken at Caterham in 1914, the engine driver with an oil can, the fireman and guard parading proudly as usual.

Standing at London Bridge is the pride of the line No. 810, sole representative of the S.E.C.R. "U" class. This was probably the most modern engine the old "Slow, Easy and Comfortable" as it was known ever possessed. They lasted right up to the end of steam haulage on British Rail. No. 810 had many Swindon features, which probably accounts for its success, including top feed on a tapered boiler carrying a pressure of 200 p.s.i. (which was an adventurous figure for the time) and long valve-travel etc. It is surrounded by a crowd of justifiably proud South Eastern men when photographed during July 1919.

A typical example of an L.B.S.C.R. signal box, Purley South, photographed in 1913.

Interior of Upper Warlingham signal box showing "Lock and Block" instruments. Hanging on the front of the shelf, attached to a wooden ball, is the key release for the latter instruments. This form of signalling was very safe, because once a train was signalled on the instrument, that train had to pass the home signal before the signal at the box behind could be lowered for the following train to leave. However, if the signalled train was unable to come as planned (it may have broken down) the key was used to unlock the instrument, thus allowing the signal in rear to be lowered again for the next train to approach. This key, essential as it was to the working, was the weak link in an otherwise foolproof system and its misuse had caused accidents. However deliberate misuse apart, "Lock and Block" was for a hundred years the safest form of traditional signalling.

No. 1 is a handsome 4-4-2 tank engine of the Belfast and Northern Counties Railway seen here at Ballynahine with a one coach train. The jack on the running plate seems hardly strong enough to support the locomotive's weight. The driver, or fireman, can be seen squatting just behind the jack carrying out a little maintenance.

Another view of this class showing the small diameter bogie wheels and "Atlantic" wheel arrangement. The photograph was taken at Newcastle in the early 1920's.

Pictured here is a three cylinder compound locomotive leaving Carlisle Citadel with a train for Leeds. No. 1006 is a Johnson cum Deeley compound built in 1905 as No. 1001 and renumbered in 1907 as No. 1006. She makes a brave sight in the strong afternoon sunshine as she sets out to tackle one of the hardest routes in the country, over the wild moors of Westmorland and the West Riding. A good deal of patient "burnishing" has gone into No. 1006's turnout, as can be seen by the "bright work" on the smoke box front and cylinder covers. Carlisle was full of colour at this time, with no less than seven companies using the station, all with their locos and rolling stock in their colourful liveries.

A "Cardean" class No. 906 is here waiting at a station on the "Caley" system, unidentified as yet but maybe a reader will recognize it and let me know where it is. These engines were the pride of the Caledonian Railway, designed by James McIntosh, the man who told Churchward of the G.W.R., that he didn't care how efficient the modern G.W.R. engines were, *he* didn't like them because "they were na' bonny!" The "Cardean" class worked most of the "crack" expresses of the line but this one appears to be at the head of a stopping train. There is more to the station than appears at first glance; a footbridge spans invisible tracks to the left and a pretty lattice-work signal shows the site of a set of facing points.

Positively glowing with colour under the roof of Edinburgh Waverley station, is the prototype of the famous "Dunalastair" class 4-4-0. This locomotive was designed by Drummond before he left to go south to the L.S.W.R. No. 721, *Dunalstair* is waiting at the head of an Edinburgh to Carlisle express, while some passengers chat to the driver.

A rather untidy "Dunalastair" class, No. 728 gets ready for the run. A shunter can be seen sneaking off round the "blind side" of the engine with a screw coupling in his hand after making some illegal shunting operations! As can be seen from the picture, No. 728 is not fitted with a proper front coupling and was not supposed to be used for shunting, hence the stealthy departure of the shunter. Having done a good deed for the station staff the enginemen now turn to the serious business of preparing for the journey. Judging from the column of smoke from the chimney the fireman is building the fire and the driver is just coming off the footplate to do some oiling. Notice the "Canopy lights" on the cabside, and the beautifully panelled Caledonian coach alongside the engine.

Although this engine is from a design seven years older than that of the 4-4-0 on page 51, there is nothing old-fashioned about its construction. Reid's "Atlantics" were highly thought of, running very fast yet so smoothly that they gave the driver, who was used to earlier less well thought out designs, a completely wrong impression of the train's speed. When they first came into service, trains hauled by them were arriving at stations well ahead of time, with complaints from passengers in the dining car about reckless speed round corners! Drivers brought up on under-powered machines had to develop a new technique for driving these powerful locomotives. This engine, No. 878 *Hazeldene*, 4-4-2 is seen here coming off a train from Edinburgh at Carlisle. Notice the very smart Horse-box with a white painted roof in the background as well as the Caley engine.

North British Railway 4-4-0 No. 287, *Glen Gyle* stands at the head of the "Lothian Coast Express", the 5.40 p.m. departure from Edinburgh Waverley. Though the engine seems to date from the eighties or nineties of the last century, it is in fact of 1913 vintage. Its designer, W. P. Ried, intended them for intermediate passenger work and for the difficult West Highland line. To this end he fitted them with what was then considered to be a small diameter wheel which was six feet exactly.

Wartime upsets many longstanding routines, and here one can see an example. This engine is a smaller version of the "Experiment" class 4-6-0's — and known as "19 goods" and is a Mixed Traffic class. A powerful 4-6-0 engine of the L.N.W.R. seen hurrying through Radley with a special south-bound train of cattle trucks, possibly the horses of some cavalry regiment bound for France. The interesting question is where did the train get onto G.W.R. metals — almost certainly not at Oxford, but perhaps from the G.C.R. *via* Woodford Halse and Banbury — at any rate it is a very unusual working. Notice that the trucks have all been white-washed to show that they have been properly cleaned since they were last used.

The famous black livery of the London and North Western Railway shows off the hard working lines of this "Precursor" class No. 2031 *Waverley*. Though known as the "Premier Line", its engines always had to be pushed hard to keep time on the long hauls to and from Carlisle and Euston especially with very heavy trains of the period. No. 2031 was photographed at Oxford, Rewley Road, within a stone's throw of the G.W.R. shed and the "Stars" that had kept the L.N.W.R. schedules with such nonchalant ease.

Although affectionately misnamed a "Jumbo", this 6'6" "Precedent" was a pillar of the L.N.W.R., performing day after day amazing feats of long distance haulage on the Anglo-Scottish expresses. Their 2-4-0 wheel arrangement makes them look somewhat antediluvian but they really did "hold the fort" on the Premier Line until the bigger "Precursor" and "Experiment" Classes came along. This "Jumbo" No. 2176 *Robert Benson* was seen and captured by Bill as it stood outside the shed at Rewley Road, Oxford.

As anyone who has read Oscar Wilde's "The Importance of Being Earnest" will know, the Brighton line was a respectable line. This was a fact well understood by the employees of the Company as the turn-out of their engines testified. Examine in detail the grooming of "B2X". Over the bogie wheels the mudguards are polished and wheel spokes gleam, all inaccessible items and difficult to clean. When built, around 1897, the engine bore the proud name of *Brunel* but now, in 1913, it has sadly lost this name. The photograph was taken outside Purley South signal box where Bill was spending the day with his friends.

In common with the people of the times these locomotives had a dignity matched with a wonderful practicality, not found in the more modern generation of people or locomotives. No. 59, an enlarged "B.2" known as class "B.4", was named *Baden-Powell* but lost this name when Mr. Marsh retired as Locomotive Engineer and Mr. Billinton took his place. Bill has caught the fireman in the act of swinging round from tender to fire-hole with a shovelful of coal. He has already put coal on the fire and turned the blower on to draw air through the fire bed, hence the column of black smoke rising from the chimney. These engines were fitted with air and vacuum brakes, as can be seen from the picture on page 55.

A lovely picture of "B2X", No. 208, in full cry on the "Southern Belle" about to raise the dust through South Croydon Station. Please observe the correct colour of smoke from the chimney, indicating that the fireman has the hottest possible fire, and in consequence there is the reassuring plume of steam from the safety valves to show a boiler at full pressure.

No. 39 *La France* was the only Brighton "Atlantic" to be named in L.B.S.C.R. days, though the remainder of the class received names after grouping when this particular engine was re-named "Hartland Point". The class was built in two groups during 1905 and 1912 and No. 39 was the middle engine of the first group. They were said to be copies of the "Atlantics" designed for the Great Northern Railway by H. N. Ivatt, greatly improving the looks of the class. Photographed on a down race special at Purley about 1913.

No. 422 *North Foreland* passing Ashdown Park Hotel between Coulsdon and the north end of Merstham tunnel on the 'Old Road' with a race special for Gatwick during June 1913.

On Saturday 14 November 1925 No. 421 South Foreland broke her trailing driven axle and lost her near-side driving wheel (seen lying by the front of the engine) near Haywards Heath up main advanced starting signal whilst working the 9.40 a.m. Worthing to Victoria express. The train was worked forward by a little 0-4-2, 'D' class suburban tank, No. 299 New Cross, while C2X class 0-6-0 No. 524 rushed up from Brighton with the crane and breakdown train.

The same accident seen head-on, giving a good view of the Brighton steam crane No. 16 and some ancient coaching stock. 'C2X' No. 524 at the rear.

'Gladstone' class No. 214 *Gladstone* passing Purley South on 31 July 1911 with the 7.15 a.m. Brighton to London Bridge express.

A good close-up view of this remarkable class is given in this picture of No. 174, unnamed at the time of this picture but once called *Fratton*. To modern eyes it seems impossible that such a machine should work long distance expresses, particularly between Victoria and Portsmouth, a route that took them through Fratton, maybe accounting for the otherwise unprepossessing name of No. 174. Out of a total of 36 built, No. 172 lasted the longest to 1933, eight others just managed to come into the beginning of the 1930's, a life span of fifty years. No. 174, standing here so quietly, seems to personify the traditional English characteristics of understatement, modestly hiding its capabilities behind a sober front, possessing in fact the same qualities as the men who designed and built it.